# HAPPINESS
*is a*
# MOVING TARGET

An Interactive Guide
*to*
Determining Your Happiness

## DON WICKER, PH.D.

authorHOUSE®

*AuthorHouse™*
*1663 Liberty Drive*
*Bloomington, IN 47403*
*www.authorhouse.com*
*Phone: 1-800-839-8640*

*Published by AuthorHouse 10/09/2014*

*ISBN: 978-1-4969-4580-8 (sc)*
*ISBN: 978-1-4969-4579-2 (e)*

*Library of Congress Control Number: 2014918079*

# Acknowledgments

To Mary Wicker, my wife and best friend in life, thanks for your continued support during this very influential endeavor. To the countless individuals that were willing to have dialog regarding this subject with me, thanks for your support. Finally, I would like to thank all of the college professors that added suggestions and comments to this book.

# Contents

# INTRODUCTION

What is happiness? According to Webster's dictionary, happiness is an agreeable feeling or condition of the soul arising from good fortune or propitious happenings of any kind; the possession of those circumstances or that state of being which is attended with enjoyment; the state of being happy; contentment; joyful satisfaction; felicity; blessedness.

In this book we will explore the true meaning of happiness. We will explore how happiness is a moving target, and how everyone seeks this emotion. As we know, having fun can create short-term happiness. Would most people recognize happiness if they did not also experience sadness? Or, maybe it's more realistic to say that most people recognize happiness because they have witnessed or experienced sadness.

Our perceptions can influence our daily happiness. In this book I describe a situation in which my wife let someone steal her happiness. She gave away her power based on her perception of a situation. The mind-set we use to interpret situations can determine whether we view them positively or negatively. Whatever happens to us, our mind-set can always change a negative situation into a positive one.

Everyone has the power to change a situation that makes them unhappy. It's an individual choice: Change it, or complain about it. I choose to change my situation to obtain or maintain happiness. But as a society we are not giving happiness enough priority. Despite decades of economic growth we are no happier now than we were sixty years ago. Employees are still working more than forty hours a week, work depression is still a problem, and employees are working jobs they do not like. We must rethink our priorities. The good news is that our actions and choices can affect our happiness. What makes us happy has less to do with our money or possessions than with our attitudes and relationships with other people.

When we are happy in the moment, sustaining that emotion is difficult; however, we must realize that happiness can't be placed in a bottle. A person can place a written note in a bottle to save for later, but saving happiness for later is impossible. In this book I analyze the process of training for happiness, which starts when we are born. As infants we cry for food, water, and attention. When our needs are fulfilled we stop crying. Normally, when a baby stops crying it's satisfied with its current situation. And satisfaction indicates happiness. This process could be considered training for adulthood; in essence, we are crying or screaming to obtain our wants and desires.

Another way to maintain happiness is to work in a job that one enjoys. Enjoyment and job satisfaction can outweigh all the more tangible job expectations, such as wages and benefits.

Its remarkable what can happen to people with the passage of time, and how we change through the years. I remember when I was a child and how happy my friends and I were. We enjoyed most everything, from playing in the sand to riding our bikes all day. Most kids are truly happy; however, something happens between childhood and adulthood. Maybe our main purpose in life is to experience only minor stints of happiness. Consider it a taste or tease; a minor sample of what is to come in the afterlife. What if happiness in the afterlife is a constant, nonstop experience—the emotion we'll feel for the rest of our existence? Is it possible? We will analyze this and other questions in this book.

Several controversial subjects will be discussed in regards to happiness, such as church and happiness, how we create our own unhappiness, and finally, how people steal our happiness.

Regarding church, our expectation is that it should make people happy or happier than they were prior to attending service. But some of the unhappiest people I have ever seen attend church. I have talked with them and witnessed their unhappiness through their behavior. Not that all church members are unhappy; however, most of them that have crossed my path were. We will analyze this subject and give you the opportunity to determine the truth for yourself.

Is it possible that people create unhappiness through the choices they make? Also, people can have their happiness stolen from them by the criminal justice system. When anger escalates to dangerous levels it can lead to destructive results, in these cases a person may be allowing someone or something to control their behavior. From DUI's to bank embezzlement, bad choices produce unhappy results over and over again. With the examples I provide in this book it's easy to see how most people create their own unhappiness.

# HAVING FUN CREATES HAPPINESS

E very action has a reaction. For every positive action there is a negative action, and vice-versa. With each action most people experience either happy emotions or sad emotions; it merely depends on the situation. Would most people recognize happiness if they did not experience sadness? Or, maybe it's more realistic to say that most people recognize happiness because they have witnessed sadness or experienced sadness.

A good example is my current marriage, in which I am the happiest I have ever been. My wife is everything I always wanted in a mate. She treats me the way I always believed a wife should treat a husband. What is the foundation for my happiness? Well, it's based on my experience of a previous marriage. Since I remarried and experienced the best of what a good marriage can offer I can truly say that I am happily married. For some people it is difficult to determine whether their marriage is happy or sad. I would say that their reference point could be missing. If someone has not been exposed to other married couples that are truly happy, or has not experienced marriage, how can that person truly recognize a happy marriage? If all of your married friends spend an average of one day a week with their spouses and they appear happy, that reference point is giving

1

false information. What people think is normal originates from their environment. If everyone in your environment appears to be happy, will your reference point be influenced? Of course it will.

What most people need to do is create fun and happiness in their lives. One way is through exercising, which connects our minds and bodies. Being active makes us happier as well as physically healthier. It instantly improves our mood and can even lift us out of depression. We don't all need to run marathons. There are simple things we can do to be more active each day. We can also boost our well-being by spending time outdoors, eating healthy, unplugging from technology, and getting enough sleep! It could be as simple as walking on the beach or through the neighborhood. Some individuals have exercise routines that consist of sit-ups and a sauna every day—just enough to make them happy and lift their spirits. Some people take Zumba dance classes twice a week, which can be fun; it's a matter of getting involved in some activities with others. While writing this book at the age of fifty-two I can still say that I am a good athlete. I utilize my local recreation center to exercise and play basketball approximately four or five times per week. I realize that exercise gives the body endorphins and makes us feel good. However, exercising is only a part of the puzzle. When we analyze our happiness related to exercise we realize the importance of relationships that we have with other gym members. I have been attending the same recreation center for the past nine years, and I recognize most members or know their names. This experience has created relationships with people working for the same "cause"—the *battle of the bulge*! These relationships connect people as if they were family members, or fighting a war together, and these connections make us happy. Most people appear to be happy while working out at the gym. Exercising is another tool that can increase our happiness factor.

Is it possible to have fun exercising? Please describe what you do to have fun during an average week.

_____

_____

_____

_____

_____

_____

_____

_____

_____

_____

_____

_____

_____

_____

_____

_____

_____

_____

# You Deserve To Be Happy

# Take My Happiness

My wife recently encountered a situation in which someone briefly took her happiness. It was the holiday season, and she had gone shopping for Christmas gifts at our local mall. She was excited and happy as she reached the mall parking lot, but as she began to look for a parking spot she started to feel stressed.

After driving around for a couple of minutes she found a good parking spot close to the main door. As she waited for the car to move out of the parking spot she felt happy again. Not only was she going shopping, she was also getting one of the best parking spots at the mall. She turned on her turn signal to inform other drivers that she was waiting for the other car to move, and then a strange thing happened; as the driver backed out, another driver from the other direction simply zoomed into the parking spot. This was clearly impolite; after all, my wife was waiting for the other driver to move, and had her turn signal on. My wife was very upset and blew her car horn several times at the other driver. She started to roll down her window to yell at this person, but decided not to and simply drove away to look for another spot.

Good decision—because another spot opened up right next to the driver that had taken her original spot—quite a coincidence. It was clear that my wife's happiness disappeared during this incident. She sat in the car and called a girlfriend to tell her about the incident, which calmed her demeanor; however, she was no longer happy, or excited about shopping. This incident seemed to take away her happiness. Can happiness really be stolen from us? How can we determine if it has occurred?

Can happiness be measured by a judge? To measure happiness, we must begin with the meaning of the word. The problem, of course, is that *happiness* is used in at least two ways. The first is as an emotion: *Were you happy yesterday?* The second is as a general evaluation: *Are you happy with your life as a whole?* The word is not one we use lightly. Happiness is an aspiration of every human being and can also be a measure of social progress. America's founding fathers declared the inalienable right to pursue happiness for everyone.

In the case of my wife's parking lot incident, something minor basically changed her emotional state. Is it possible to maintain happiness when confronting adversity? What would you do to maintain your happiness in this situation? Please describe.

_____

_____

_____

_____

_____

_____

_____

_____

_____

_____

_____

_____

_____

_____

_____

_____

_____

_____

# You Deserve To Be Happy

# Moving and Happiness

I t's amazing to think of what makes a person happy. It appears we are happy with the thought of being happy. Most people are told how to be happy by spouses, friends, or family members. There has always been an endless supply of information on how to make people happier.

After working for thirty or thirty-five years, most people look forward to retiring, and they are told that retirement will make them happy. It seems that people always believe they will be happy if they engage in an activity that is the opposite of what they are currently doing. While working day after day, year after year, people imagine how nice it would be not to work, and to live for themselves, not needing to awaken early in the morning or stay at work late every night. It sounds like something that could make anyone happy.

But when we are not working it's often the opposite; we believe working will make us happy. Unemployed people would do almost anything to obtain a job. Depending on the duration of their unemployment, most out-of-work people believe that working will make them happy. It appears that every action we take in life provokes a counter action. When we are working we wish we were not; when we are off of work we wish we were working. Some married people wish they were single; some single people wish they were married. Extremely thin people wish they were healthy and could gain a little weight; overweight people wish they were thin. Some famous people wish they could walk down the street without being recognized; people who are not famous wish they were famous enough to be recognized while walking down the street. It's always something that people desire; unfortunately, we usually want the opposite of what we currently have. This opposite desire is usually constant throughout life regarding products or other tangible things. For example, if we have a small car we usually want a larger car; and after we have owned a large car with poor gas mileage for many years, we want to trade it for a small car. Most people that have owned large houses for years will tell you that they are tired of the maintenance and of the cleaning these houses require. They want to downsize and purchase smaller homes. And as we know, people with small houses usually want larger houses.

Why do people always want something they do not have? Usually they have been told that happiness will arrive if they get what they don't have.

It does not matter what we currently own, or our economic status. There is always a commercial or media story telling us that we will be happy when we obtain something more or change our status.

Why do we change? Apparently we change because we are all searching for happiness. We are exposed to thousands of media stories and people telling us what will make us happy. We are bombarded, as I mentioned earlier, with messages about what it takes to be happy. Do we believe these messages? Absolutely! If we didn't, our economy would stop moving forward, stagnation would result, and our society would totally collapse.

Can we imagine a world where nothing ever changes, where people stop desiring things? Normally we want things to make us happy, things we see in our everyday lives. No one is perfect; however, we sometimes compare a negative view of ourselves with an unrealistic view of other people. Dwelling on our flaws, concentrating on what we are not rather than what we've got, can make it harder to be happy. Learning to accept and be kinder to ourselves when things go wrong will increase our enjoyment of life, our resilience, and our well-being. Happiness is a moving target. And I can say from experience that moving from location to location does not increase happiness; however, it is what most people do in their search for happiness. During the earlier stages of my career with General Motors Corporation I moved six times—from Michigan to San Francisco; from San Francisco to Dallas; from Dallas to Michigan; from Michigan to Los Angeles; and finally, from Los Angles to Lubbock, Texas. With each move, I hoped that it would make me and my family happier. But did it? Actually, what I experienced was more stress.

During each of these moves I expected increased happiness; however, what I really experienced was stress. Establishing a new house, finding a new school for the kids, meeting new friends and co-workers, getting comfortable with a new area—it was all stressful. How could I, or anyone, think that moving could bring happiness? I believe most people think they will improve their lives by moving. Our ideas of happiness are usually more enjoyable than our actual experiences. A perfect example is my current situation. I live in a beach community. I can see the water at the beach from my deck. It appears to be a great community; however, no matter what my situation is, I believe improvement is possible. I now want to move out of this community due to restrictions the city imposes on property improvements. No one likes to be controlled, and I am no exception. I am currently searching for a community where I can be in total control of my property. I think it's due to my strong *locus of control*. This term indicates the degree to which individuals believe they can control events affecting them. Individuals who have a high internal locus of control believe that their own behavior and actions primarily, but not necessarily totally, determine many of the events in their lives. On the other hand, individuals who have a high external locus of control believe that chance, fate, or other individuals primarily determine their happiness. Locus of control is typically considered to be a part of the conscientiousness factor. Many differences between internal locus of control and external locus of control are significant in explaining aspects of behavior in organizations and other social settings. Internal individuals control their own behavior better, are more active politically and socially, and seek information about their situations more actively than do external individuals. Compared to externals, internals are more likely to try to influence or persuade others and are less likely to be influenced by others. Internals often are more achievement-oriented than externals. Compared to internals, externals appear to prefer a more structured, directive style of supervision. The more control you have in your life the happier you are.

Why should people stay in a situation where happiness is absent? What is the benefit? If a situation is not making you happy, change it! All people have the power to change situations that make them unhappy, it's an individual choice. Change it, or complain about it. I choose to change my situation to obtain or maintain happiness. Complaining will not give me the results I desire.

Did you ever anticipate happiness because of moving from one location to another? Please describe such a time.

_____

_____

_____

_____

_____

_____

_____

_____

_____

_____

_____

_____

_____

_____

_____

_____

_____

_____

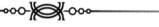

# You Deserve To Be Happy

# Society and
# Happiness

What if we did not have the media or individuals telling us what we need to be happy? Let's analyze our thoughts for a moment. Most of our desires originate from our thoughts, and our thoughts are developed by our environments. Where would society be if we had no desires or needs?

We all want to lead happy lives, and want the people we love to be happy too. But as a society we are not giving happiness enough priority. Despite decades of economic growth we are no happier now than we were sixty years ago. We need to rethink our priorities. The good news is that our actions and choices can affect our happiness. What makes us happy has less to do with our money and possessions than with our attitudes and relationships with other people.

People who have meaning and purpose in their lives are happier. They feel more in control, and get more out of life. They also experience less stress, anxiety and depression. But where do we find meaning and purpose? It might come from doing a job that makes a difference, from religion or spiritual beliefs, or from family. The answers vary for each of us, but they all involve being connected to something bigger than ourselves. We must be motivated to move in a happy direction. As I stated in one of my previous books, *Motivation*, what motivates one person may be a de-motivator for others. What one person views as a de-motivator may be a motivator to others. Most of us have witnessed dramatic examples of motivation throughout our lives. We've seen brothers and sisters who grew up in the same households with the same parents achieve opposite outcomes. One sibling becomes CEO of a company, and the other becomes a below-average employee moving from company to company. How do we discern the true motivating forces within each individual? Are we all motivated to find happiness?

If we analyze the term *motivation* more closely, we will discover that it is a continuous process that occurs in our brains on a daily basis. We are motivated throughout our days to accomplish tasks or complete activities. Our chief motivator lies within our inner thoughts. What we think about becomes a driving force for our entire existence. The course of our daily lives is determined by our thought processes. For example, if a person thinks about eating food all day while working, what do you think will happen once work is finished? The person will probably experience the enjoyment of a big meal, perhaps at some nice restaurant.

Society and culture have always played a major part in our happiness. Our understanding of culture can be summarized into five elements: Culture is *learned*, not innate; people are socialized from childhood to learn the rules and norms of their culture. It also means it is possible to learn a new culture. Culture is *shared*, meaning that the focus is on things common to the members of the group rather than on individual differences. This makes it possible to study and identify group patterns. Culture is *compelling*, meaning that specific behavior is determined by culture without individuals being aware of its influence. This makes it important to understand culture in order to understand a behavior. Culture is an *interrelated* set, meaning that while various facets can be examined in isolation, they should be understood in the context of the whole; so, a culture must be studied as a complete entity. Culture provides *orientation* to people, meaning that members of a particular group generally react in the same way to a given stimulus. This means that understanding a culture can help in determining how group members might react in various situations.

Can a person really find happiness within society? Please describe the happiness you have found within society.

_____

_____

_____

_____

_____

_____

_____

_____

_____

_____

_____

_____

_____

_____

_____

_____

_____

_____

# You Deserve To Be Happy

# STORIES ABOUT
# HAPPINESS

Once there was a man named Bob, making a very modest living working as an accountant, working only four hours per day. When he was not working he spent his time with family and friends, or fishing. He especially enjoyed spending time with his wife and daughter, and viewed these moments as priceless. He treasured the opportunity to play with his daughter and the prospect of growing old with his wife – even as he recognized that most working men didn't have such luxuries.

He also enjoyed spending time with friends—not doing anything special, just sitting around talking or playing cards. Lastly, he loved to fish for his family. When I say *fishing for his family*, I mean catching fish for the family dinner. He would spend a couple of hours each day fishing, maybe catching seven fish. Catching seven fish was average for his two hours of fishing. He only fished for two hours because that was all he needed. Then one day while fishing he noticed another man near his fishing hole. This man, who happened to be a Harvard graduate and businessman, introduced himself. The fisherman said that he came to this area every day to fish. The man asked how many fish he had caught. The fisherman stated that he came to this location every day for two hours. The businessman from Harvard inquired as to how many fish he normally caught in those two hours. The fisherman stated that he usually caught seven fish, just enough to feed his family.

The man from Harvard asked, "Why don't you stay for eight hours and catch twenty-eight fish"?

The fisherman said, "Wow! And then, what?"

"You could continue to expand your business and sell the fish."

"Wow! And then what?"

"You could hire other people to help you sell the fish."

"Wow! And then what?"

"One day you could make enough money to open up your own fish store."

"Wow! And then what?"

"Your business could be so successful that you could sell it for a large sum of money."

"Wow! And then what?"

"You could retire and enjoy your life."

"Wow! And then what?"

"Sit back and spend time with your family and friends—and maybe do some fishing."

"Wow! "Isn't that where I started?"

Obviously, we must remember that always needing more is not a prescription for happiness. You may already be happy, but blind to the reality of your situation. Analyze your situation and revisit the scenario I just described. Apply my example to your current life situation. Are you happy? Can we really say that the key to happiness is money? Because in the scenario I described, the Harvard businessman's mind-set was that money brings happiness. The fisherman believed that enjoying his family and free time was all the happiness he needed. Apparently the Harvard businessman needed money to enjoy the simpler things in life, whereas the fisherman was living a simple happy life already.

Can you remember a situation where someone offered suggestions that would improve your life? Please describe how you changed based on these suggestions.

_____

_____

_____

_____

_____

_____

_____

_____

_____

_____

_____

_____

_____

_____

_____

_____

_____

_____

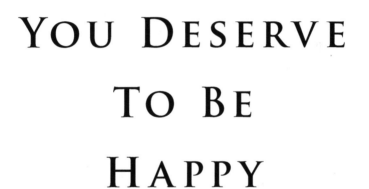

# YOU DESERVE
# TO BE
# HAPPY

# WHAT MAKES
# PEOPLE HAPPY

I s it possible to put happiness into a bottle and save it? One can actually write a note and place it into a bottle, but we cannot place happiness in a bottle for later use. One activity that seems to make people happy for a period of time is a day at the beach. During a recent visit to the beach I saw people who seemed very joyous. They were smiling, laughing, and being very friendly and courteous to each other. Maybe this atmosphere was due to a mind-set of happiness. Everyone that goes to the beach expects to experience some type of enjoyment or happiness. I do not think people go to the beach expecting to have a terrible day. In our minds we associate fun on the beach with pleasure. Is it possible to associate other things with happiness? For example, could we train our minds to find happiness working as dentists, accountants, or nurses?

It appears that our minds are trained for happiness. We are the chief trainers of our minds. We tell ourselves throughout our lives what makes us happy, and we are the deciding factor of our happiness. Whatever circumstance we encounter, we have predetermined whether we will be happy or sad.

What is happiness? A wife, a husband, or some type of event? Why can't anyone clearly define happiness? I have a perfect example of what sounds like happiness. I was listening to the radio one day and found out that one of my favorite radio personalities had got divorced. I am sure other fans and listeners were very surprised to hear about the breakup. Just the previous year, this radio personality had told listeners how happy he was in his marriage—the things he had in common with his wife, the exciting trips they experienced, and their overall joy. So his divorce was a total surprise; most fans presumed they were happy based on their perceptions. When we read or hear information, we are usually not in a position to verify details. We tend to simply believe what someone else is reporting regarding the happiness of others. Therefore trying to understand what happened to this radio personality's marriage is hard. It is our human nature to care. Caring about others is fundamental to our happiness. Helping other people is not only good for them; it's good for us, too. It makes us happier and can improve our health. Giving also creates stronger connections between people and helps to build a happier society for everyone. It's not all about money; we can also give our time, ideas, and energy. So, if you want to feel good do something good for others. Build positive relationships and connections. Relationships with other people are important. When they are strong and healthy we live longer. Our close relationships with family and friends give our lives meaning, provide support, and increase our feelings of self-worth. Our broader social networks bring a sense of belonging. So it's vital that we take action to strengthen our relationships and make new connections.

Are extended family connections in the same category as other relationships? When we spend time with our families or extended families does it create happiness? I am sure that circumstances differ from person to person. However, most people will say that spending time with family creates happy memories. I believe it has to do with being in the physical presence of people you have shared so much of your life with. It also may vary depending on how often your family or extended family gets together. In my situation, I live in a different state from my extended family. Therefore, going to visit my extended family is always a happy event. We share old and current stories and create new happy memories. I believe time away from family enhances the happiness factor.

Another factor that enhances the happiness experience is the *amount* of time spent with family. If it's a short period of time, rather than long, the experience will be enhanced. A shorter time span will decrease your happiness compared with a longer one.

Let's analyze this theory in the area of family. Some families argue all the time and never experience happiness with each other. Why does this occur? We understand how environment influences our behavior; however, the frequency of interactions can affect our happiness level. If extended families spend every weekend together bickering and discussing issues, their happiness will be decreased. If they feel they are *required* to spend family time together, that can have a negative overall effect.

Can you think of any situations in which people are happy or unhappy while spending family time together? Please describe what you believe makes people happy or unhappy during family outings.

_____

_____

_____

_____

_____

_____

_____

_____

_____

_____

_____

_____

_____

_____

_____

_____

_____

# You Deserve
# To Be
# Happy

# TRAINING FOR HAPPINESS

Are humans trained to be happy? Our training starts when we are born. We cry for food, water, and attention. When our needs are met we stop crying. Normally when a baby stops crying it's satisfied with its current situation. And usually, satisfaction indicates happiness. This process could be considered training for adulthood; in essence, we learn to cry or scream to obtain our wants and desires. It is excellent training; if you analyze the dynamics of this process, we are truly training ourselves to be happy. When we analyze the behavior of adults we observe that most people feel happy when they purchase things: homes, cars, jobs, appliances, furniture, etc.

You may be wondering *how long does this period of happiness last?* Well, let's analyze the behavior of someone purchasing a car. The first thing that happens is a person develops a *desire* for a car, perhaps through a comment from a friend, or because the current car has engine problems. Once desire starts it's similar to watching one's favorite sports team win a game. When you are watching your favorite team you anticipate them winning; you watch the entire game on the edge of your seat. Your desire is to witness your team winning the game.

You cheer and yell for each successful play, and when your team calls a timeout your excitement continues to build. As the game is close to ending and your team is winning it's hard to contain yourself. You simply want the game to stop, with your team as the winner; however, another timeout is called before the game continues. You're sure your team is going to win; you can't seem to walk away until you witness it. You shout, "Start the game!" At this point you become extremely excited. The timeout ends and the game continues.

That intense desire to see your team win shows how having goals can be another way to become happier.

The same is true when purchasing a new car. Sometimes anticipation builds for weeks or months. The thought of purchasing never leaves your mind, as media enticements continue. And the desire will not stop until you make the purchase. Feeling good about the future is important for our happiness. We all need goals to motivate us. They should be challenging enough to excite us, but also achievable. Attempting the impossible creates unnecessary stress which will decrease happiness. Choosing meaningful but realistic goals gives our lives direction. And when we achieve them we experience a sense of accomplishment and satisfaction, resulting in increased happiness.

Most people have times of stress, loss, failure, or trauma in their lives. How we respond to these events has a big impact on our well-being and happiness. We often cannot choose what happens to us, but we can choose how we react to it. Yes, in practice it's not easy, but one of the most exciting findings from recent research is that resilience, like many other life skills, can be learned. In a book written by Jonathan Haidt, "The Happiness Hypothesis", he describes "adversity hypothesis"—the idea that people need adversity, setbacks, and perhaps even trauma, to reach the highest level of strength, fulfillment, and personal development. These can lead to added happiness. The adversity hypothesis has a weak and strong version. According to the weak version, adversity can lead to growth, strength, joy, and self-improvement. The strong version is more unsettling. It contends that people *must* endure adversity to grow, and that the highest levels of growth and development are open to those who have faced and overcome great adversity. If the stronger version of the hypothesis is valid, it has profound implications for how we should live our lives and structure our societies. It also means that we should take more chances and suffer more defeats to acquire happiness.

Can individuals really be trained to be happy? Please describe situations where you have been trained to experience happiness.

_____

_____

_____

_____

_____

_____

_____

_____

_____

_____

_____

_____

_____

_____

_____

_____

_____

# You Deserve To Be Happy

# Happy Employees

Recently the following headline appeared in USA Today: "Why is Amazon paying workers up to $5,000 to quit?"

Amazon.com, Inc. is an American international electronic commerce company with headquarters in Seattle, Washington. It is the world's largest online retailer. Amazon.com started as an online bookstore, but soon diversified, selling DVDs, VHS tapes, CDs, video and audio downloads and streaming, software, video games, electronics, apparel, furniture, food, toys, and jewelry. The company also produces consumer electronics—notably the Fire Phone, Amazon Kindle e-book reader and the Kindle Fire tablet computer. Amazon is also a major provider of cloud computing services.

Amazon.com hopes the workers in its scores of fulfillment centers across the USA are happy in their jobs. But if they're not and would rather be doing something else, Amazon has a deal to offer. The company will pay them a bonus of up to $5,000 to leave. In a program that Amazon calls *Pay to Quit*, those who aren't committed to their jobs are urged to leave on their own and can get $2,000 in severance pay in the first year of employment with the bonus topping out at $5,000 in the fourth year. Therefore, employees with more than four years on the job will receive $5,000. The goal is to encourage folks to take a moment and think about what they really want. In the long run, an employee staying somewhere he or she doesn't want to be isn't healthy for the employee or the company. Having employees that are satisfied with their jobs will result in a happier workforce. Also, learning new things at work will affect their well-being in lots of positive ways. It exposes them to new ideas and helps them stay curious and engaged. It also gives them a sense of accomplishment and helps boost their self-confidence and resilience. There are many ways to learn new things throughout life—and not just formal avenues. We can share a skill with friends, join a club, learn to sing, learn to play a new sport, and so much more. Employers love it when employees have a positive approach to their work. Positive emotions like joy, gratitude, contentment, inspiration, and pride don't just feel good when we experience them. These emotions help us perform better, broaden our perception, increase our resilience, and improve our physical health. Although we need to be realistic about life's ups and downs, it helps to focus on the good aspects of any situation. As you probably know, research has shown that happy workers perform better on the job.

People are multilevel systems in another way: They are physical objects (bodies and brains) from which minds somehow emerge. And from our minds, somehow societies and cultures form. To understand ourselves fully we must study all three levels—physical, psychological, and sociocultural.

There has long been a division of academic labor. Biologists studied the brain as a physical object, psychologists studied the mind, and sociologists and anthropologists studied the socially-constructed environments within which minds develop and function. But a division of labor is productive only when the tasks are coherent, when all lines of work eventually combine to make something greater than the sum of their parts. For much of the twentieth century that didn't' happen. Each field ignored the others and focused on its own questions. But nowadays cross-disciplinary work is flourishing, spreading out from the middle level (psychology) along bridges (or perhaps ladders) down to the physical level (for example, the field of cognitive neuroscience) and up to the sociocultural level (for example, cultural psychology). The sciences are linking up, generating cross-level coherence. And, like magic, big new ideas are beginning to emerge. One of the most-profound ideas to come from the ongoing synthesis, people gain a sense of meaning when their lives cross these three levels of existence.

As I stated in my previous book, *Job Satisfaction*, happiness in one's work life requires job satisfaction. This is a sense of inner fulfillment and pride achieved when performing a particular job. It occurs when an employee feels he or she has accomplished something of importance and value, worthy of recognition. According to Webster's dictionary 3rd edition 2010, job satisfaction brings a pleasurable emotional state to the worker, which often leads to a positive work attitude and improved performance. A satisfied worker is more likely to be creative, flexible, innovative, happy, and loyal.

Selecting the correct job or position should be a priority for everyone, regardless of gender. In years past, some employees worked solely for pay and benefits, forgoing job satisfaction. However, many people now understand that employment should offer satisfaction as well. The *psychological contract* between employees and employers has changed. This refers to the unwritten expectations employees and employers have about the nature of their work relationships. At one time, employees expected to exchange their efforts and capabilities for a secure job that offered rising pay, good benefits, and career progression within the organization. But as organizations have downsized and fired workers who have given long and loyal service, a growing number of employees question whether they should be loyal to their employers.

Employers' expectations have also changed. Rather than just paying employees to follow orders and put in time, employers increasingly expect their employees to improve their knowledge, skills, and abilities. That's why it's extremely important that employees *and* employers look more closely at job satisfaction. Enjoyment and job satisfaction can outweigh all tangible job expectations, such as wages and benefits. If employers want good employees they should pay attention to job satisfaction.

Do you believe companies are searching for happy employees? Please describe situations where you have recognized that companies valued happy employees versus unhappy employees.

_____

_____

_____

_____

_____

_____

_____

_____

_____

_____

_____

_____

_____

_____

_____

_____

_____

_____

# You Deserve To Be Happy

# Happy Childhood vs Adulthood

What happens to people? How do we change throughout the years? I remember how happy my friends and I were as children. We enjoyed most everything, from playing in the sand to riding our bikes all day. Most kids are truly happy. But what happens between childhood and adulthood? As most people know, reality will eventually assert itself in everyone's life—meaning that life has a tendency to become gradually more difficult. Example: Over the years most every child attends grade school, middle school, high school, and hopefully, college. As we know, each level becomes more and more difficult. Kids start out by playing with cars and dolls in grade school, but by high school could be taking *introduction to statistics*. As we know, taking a course such as statistics can make anyone unhappy. Let's analyze the gradual change that people experience from being happy all the time to being unhappy most of the time.

Is it possible to change our present mind-sets to experience the same joy that we experienced in our younger years? It could simply be a matter of doing or experiencing some of the same things we enjoyed as kids—such as playing baseball or tennis, attending concerts, or going to the beach to play in the sand.

We can also play with our kids or pets to experience happiness. In fact, every memory we have of happiness was previously experienced. We are creatures of habit; what we remember is what we have experienced in our past.

Have you ever felt there must be more to life than what you are currently experiencing? Well, good news—there is! And it's right here in front of us. We just need to stop and take notice. Learning to be more mindful and aware does wonders for our well-being, whether it's on our walk to work, the way we eat, or in our relationships. It helps us get in tune with our feelings and stops us from dwelling on the past or worrying about the future, so we get more out of our day-to-day activities.

When my daughter was young, the friends she played with inspired happiness. It really did not matter what they were doing; they simply needed to interact with each other. Interaction was a common link and norm for my daughter's childhood happiness. However, during her tween and teen years, everything changed. Kids at this age seem to be happy when they are talking and interacting with friends. My daughter and her friends could talk all day about boys. I'm not sure whether this is caused by simple curiosity or the differences that exist between girls and boys. It seems that kids in school find it difficult to concentrate on schoolwork when the opposite sex is around, or when they're interacting or talking to them. As I stated earlier, happiness can have a powerful effect on our everyday behavior. Don't misunderstand; I'm not saying my daughter and her friends are not having fun in other ways, only that their happiness is enhanced when they are talking about boys or interacting with each other. Maybe what we learn regarding the opposite sex during our formative years stays in our consciousness throughout life. Most single people continue to search throughout their lives for a significant mate. Why? Because at an early age they learned that relationships lead to happiness. Unfortunately, divorce rates in America have increased at an astonishing rate. I believe people today are looking for happiness; therefore, they are no longer settling for unhappy relationships. Why should they? Everyone deserves to be happy.

In years past it was common to hear of marriages lasting forty, fifty, or sixty years. Many of these marriages were unhappy. Years of unhappiness—why? I truly believe, and have witnessed in our society, that people did not believe they deserved to be happy. When people are young they desire happiness. When they are old, happiness seldom visits. Why? It appears that we have been conditioned to believe that we don't deserve happiness. I was raised during a time when very few couples got divorced. Happiness and marriage were very seldom connected. I remember countless marriages that existed only on paper, happiness was not a factor. The marriage contract was the important thing. Happiness and marriage were difficult to achieve at the same time during this era. And most people did not believe they deserved happiness. If we observe life in the *21st-century*, most people believe we all deserve to be happy. Statistics show that the divorce rate is increasing. And it will continue to increase because the mind-set of most people is changing. People are starting to understand that we all deserve to be happy. Life is too short to spend in an unhappy marriage simply because our forebears accepted that as the norm.

Can a person love childhood and hate adulthood? Please describe a case in which you loved childhood situations but hated the same situations in adulthood.

_____

_____

_____

_____

_____

_____

_____

_____

_____

_____

_____

_____

_____

_____

_____

_____

_____

_____

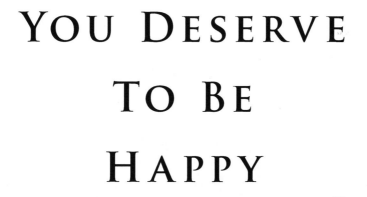

# You Deserve
# To Be
# Happy

# Happiness and the Afterlife

Maybe our main purpose is to experience only minor periods of happiness. Consider it a taste, only a little sample of what is to come in the afterlife. Perhaps in the afterlife we will truly understand happiness. What if happiness in the afterlife is a constant experience—something that continues forever? Happiness would be the only emotion we feel for the rest of our existence. Is it possible? If happiness in the afterlife is a constant, that would explain many things in our current world—especially, why everyone is constantly pursuing happiness. I know many people are happy most of the time; however, I do not know anyone that is happy 100 percent of the time. I can only imagine the excitement that constant happiness could produce. There would definitely be no need to ask people how they were doing or how their day was progressing. Happiness would be the only emotion and feeling.

Let's explore this for a moment. What about this concept we call *want* or *need*? Do we experience happiness when we want something—a new car, a new house, a new spouse? No, actually we experience unhappiness. Our desires do not help us feel good; in fact, they make us feel bad. Happiness cannot occur when we want or need something. But we are too consumed in our own mind-sets to understand what forces are working in our subconscious minds to create unhappiness. Therefore, our subconscious minds can never be completely happy; we are always looking or striving for something. Regardless of whom we are or what we think, our minds make us want more, more, and more. When we feel bad we want to feel good. When we eat too much we want to stop eating. When we do not eat we want to eat. When we are tired we desire sleep. All of our actions are geared toward improvement, fulfilling our desires, or achieving happiness. When was the last time one of your friends was complaining about a partner or spouse—only to be separated years later and then complain about *not* having a partner or spouse? It, may be that people love to complain, or are simply always striving for happiness.

If a person did not desire happiness he or she would not take action. It is apparent that happiness or the desire for it moves the world forward. In the entire spectrum of life many different things make people happy. Some people are happy with a new car, a new purse, a new house, or a new job. I am sure most of us can remember how we felt when we purchased a new car. But how long does that happiness last? Happiness can last forever if we choose to be happy.

Have you ever felt that happiness only exists in your mind? Please describe the last time you experienced happiness in your subconscious mind.

_____

_____

_____

_____

_____

_____

_____

_____

_____

_____

_____

_____

_____

_____

_____

_____

_____

# You Deserve To Be Happy

# CHURCH AND
# HAPPINESS

D oes Church make people happy or sad? Well, if you ask
the average parishioner or church member I am sure the
majority of them will tell you that they go to church expecting
to gain additional happiness in their lives. I can honestly say
from my personal experience growing up as a preacher's kid,
attending church services two or three times per week does
not automatically bring happiness. People I observed in this
environment were not happier than people in the secular world.
Our expectation is that church should make people happy or
happier than they were prior to attending service. But some of
the unhappiest people I have ever seen attend church regularly.
Not that all church members are unhappy, but the majority that
have crossed my path were. I always asked myself why this was
so. Was it that they were searching for something that was not
there? Maybe they were expecting church or God to give them
a total happiness transformation that would last a lifetime.

If we analyze the mentality of church members we can
understand why they are looking for love and happiness. It's
something they expect with God in the afterlife; therefore, the
closer they get to God the happier they should become. But
the search for happiness continues. Some people believe that

a church is similar to a hospital. People go to a hospital to get well; some go to the church to get happy. With singing and praying, it would seem to be the perfect place to find happiness. But can people really find happiness in a building before they find it within themselves? As I stated previously, happiness does not often last an entire day; usually it only occurs for a short time. In fact, happiness is sporadic and infrequent at best. The average person spends a fraction of their time at church, and most cannot find happiness there because they're unhappy within themselves.

As we have learned, attending religious services or church is one of the most common ways that people seek to enhance their relationships with God and find true happiness. When we worship, pray, and study our Bibles with others in a community of trust, we gain tremendous social support. Many people don't have friends outside of church. When people meet with close friends on a regular basis, work together as a group, and participate in meaningful activities, they form a happiness bond. At the same time, they share a certain social identity, a sense of belonging to a moral faith community. This sense of belonging seems to be the key to the relationship between church attendance and life satisfaction.

Have you ever felt that church should be associated with happiness? Please describe a situation where church was associated with happiness in your life.

_____

_____

_____

_____

_____

_____

_____

_____

_____

_____

_____

_____

_____

_____

_____

_____

_____

# You Deserve To Be Happy

# WE CREATE
# UNHAPPINESS

O ver the years I have had the opportunity to sit in a
courtroom and observe courtroom procedures. As we
know, a judge is a person who has the authority to hear and
decide court cases or to make assessments about things. Other
than television court judges I have never witnessed a judge
expressing happiness. Think about what it takes to be a judge:
attending school for years, fighting cases, arguing with clients,
studying for the bar exams, and spending years in training.
One would think a person who had expended such effort would
be very happy with the status of a judge. Attaining the status
of a judge may be a happy experience. But the daily task of
judging is not. We also believe that someone in these types of
positions should not be happy. I mentioned television judges
earlier; when we watch them smiling and laughing, we view it
as entertainment. It does not seem realistic; the judges on these
shows look like they are having a good time. Why can't real
lawyers or judges have a similar experience? After all, they've
studied and trained for years for the opportunity to attain these
positions. Why not be happy?

Regardless of how happy a person is, sadness can occur
anytime. Most people can identify what makes them sad.

When we receive a traffic ticket for speeding we feel sad. When someone we know dies, or gets hurt in an accident we are sad. When a close friend or family member moves away we are sad. You may be wondering why it is so easy to identify sadness versus happiness. It's as if we spend the majority of our lives being sad. Let's analyze this situation. There are twenty-four hours in a day; the average person spends two of those hours being happy. How do I know this? Well, I can analyze my own life to obtain data. For instance, I spend eight hours sleeping, which leaves sixteen hours for waking activities. I spend two hours exercising, two hours eating, four hours watching TV or listening to music, two hours driving to work and taking my daughter to her activities, two hours showering and using the bathroom, one hour reading, one hour preparing for work, and the two remaining hours in activities devoted to my own happiness.

Wow! Two hours for happiness. Sounds like we live in an unhappy world! Therefore, it's up to us to seek out happy opportunities every day. Remember, if you're like me, you only have two hours available each day to seek happiness. Therefore we must deliberately incorporate happiness into our daily activities.

What types of jobs would most people consider happy jobs, and what types would be considered unhappy?

The following is a list I compiled from Internet research, including data from Forbesmanagement.com2013, along with my opinions regarding happy jobs and unhappy jobs.

| **Happy Jobs** | **Unhappy Jobs** |
|---|---|
| College professor | Judge/Lawyer |
| Real estate agent | Accountant |
| Quality engineer | Associate attorney |

Senior sales representative

Construction superintendent

Senior application developer

Executive administrative
assistant

Human resource manager

Network engineer

General manager

Consultant

Property manager

Customer service associate

Clerk

Registered nurse

Landscaper

Garbage collector

Legal assistant

Pharmacy technician

Technical support specialist

Case manager

## HAPPY JOBS DEFINED

**College professor.** A scholarly teacher. The precise meaning of the term varies by country. Literally, *professor* derives from Latin as a "person who professes", being usually an expert in arts or sciences, a teacher of the highest rank.

**Real estate agent.** A person who represents buyers or sellers in the transfer of real property. This is the person on the front lines of the real estate market, who performs such tasks as showing homes to perspective buyers and negotiating transactions on behalf of clients.

**Quality Engineer.** Monitors and audits the quality of manufactured goods in any of various industries, including the automobile, textile, clothing, food and electronics industries. Works to find defects, identify their causes, and develop solutions.

**Senior Sales Representative.** Generates sales by promoting products from manufacturers or wholesalers to customers. May work for manufacturers, wholesalers or technical companies, and may sell a wide range of products, such as electronics, clothing, or food. A representative's previous sales record is usually the most important factor in securing a senior sales representative position, but employers usually prefer candidates with a college degree and technical knowledge.

---

- What is the common element in the happy jobs category?

---

## Unhappy Jobs Defined

**Judge.** The judge's first role is to make sure all the parties and witnesses follow proper courtroom procedure. Although this doesn't sound particularly exciting, procedure is of vital importance to the legal system. It was designed to ensure that everyone who comes to court gets a fair trial.

**Lawyer.** This person interprets the law through actions and words for the protection of an individual, a business concern or an idea. A lawyer must be widely versed in many areas. The education of lawyers never ends because they must constantly stay abreast of information which may be of use to clients.

**Accountant.** The accountant is responsible for systematic and comprehensive recording of financial transactions pertaining to businesses. *Accounting* also refers to the process of summarizing, analyzing and reporting these transactions. The financial statements that summarize a large company's operations, financial position and cash flows over a particular period are a concise summary of all the financial transactions it has entered into over this period. Accounting is one of the key functions for almost any business; it may be handled by a bookkeeper or accountant at a small firm, or by an entire department with dozens of employees at a larger company.

**Associate Attorney.** This is typically a subordinate coworker of another attorney. In general, a business *associate* is a person or organization distinct from the primary entity's workforce. In the legal field, *associate* often refers to an attorney who has not been made a partner to the law firm.

---

• What is the common element in the unhappy jobs category?

---

All of the jobs listed are based on strong emotions and attitudes. As I stated in my previous book, *Attitude is # 1,* attitude can be the determining factor to our happiness. Can you remember attempting to turn a negative situation into a positive one when you had a job that you disliked? Maybe you need to think back to your childhood days or to your very first job. If you are like me, I'm sure you worked jobs just to make a buck or to show your parents that you were responsible. My jobs were no different from those of many other adolescents; I was a landscaper, maintenance worker, furniture mover, and security guard. These weren't the best jobs in the world, but I enjoyed all of them. I would have to say that my enjoyment originated with my positive attitude.

Yes, attitude is king. When I worked as a landscaper I was determined to keep a positive outlook. As everyone knows, pushing a heavy lawnmower can be very tiring. So my job became a full-time work-out, benefitting my body and mind. I changed my attitude, turning what could have been a negative into a positive. My attitude toward this job made a 360-degree turn. My job became a mandatory workout with significant benefits. I would look forward to going to work each day. I knew that I would gain strength in my arms and legs, which would help me in sports. I controlled my perception and outlook regarding events. At one time my attitude became so positive that I thought it was humorous that my employer was paying me to get a complete workout every day. Of course, a negative attitude in this situation could have destroyed my will to work. A negative attitude in a job such as landscaping could make a person reluctant to come to work. It might affect performance and eagerness to get the job done.

One positive side to a negative attitude is that it can always be changed. Attitudes are generally positive or negative views of a person, place, thing, or event. Unlike personality, attitudes are expected to change as a function of experience.

One way to ensure a negative attitude is to create circumstances that we know will make us unhappy. For example, suppose we're earning a salary that allows us to pay bills and enjoy good quality and leisure time with our families. Then we trade that situation for a more stressful job with greater responsibility, additional work hours that allow for only limited leisure time with family, stressful travel from state to state causing health issues. But, I almost forgot—we're making more money. And as we know, most people think money is the path to happiness.

Is it possible to create our own unhappiness? Please describe
situations where you did this.

_____

_____

_____

_____

_____

_____

_____

_____

_____

_____

_____

_____

_____

_____

_____

_____

_____

_____

# You Deserve To Be Happy

# CHILDREN INSPIRE HAPPINESS

While I was sitting at my local coffee shop drinking coffee, a lady entered with two adorable children. It was as if a light turned on for all of the customers. Most of the ladies in the coffee shop made smiley faces and mentioned how pretty the children were. I even felt myself smiling uncontrollably. As other customers walked into the coffee shop they simply had to touch, smile, or comment to the mother about her adorable children. While sitting there drinking my coffee I had to ponder the thought: Do children inspire people to be happy? I believe there is some truth to this notion. I can think back to the times when my kids were very young, and we always seemed to get similar reactions.

Is it the innocence of children that makes us happy—the fun we see them having that we once experienced ourselves? I think it's more that we see in them our own past lives. Most parents try to live their lives through their children. Some children swim or join baseball teams for their parents' enjoyment. Most parents enjoy the experience their children are having. For example, I recently took my family to an Amusement Park. As most people know, amusement parks are designed for families to have fun. With countless rides and activities, they allow families to be in continuous motion. I am not much fun when it comes to riding roller coasters, so I decided to take a break while my wife, daughter, and daughter's friend took the challenge. During my break I observed countless families enjoying themselves in the park. Most of the time it appeared that children were telling their parents about the fun they were having on the rides. From roller coasters to Ferris wheels, the excitement these rides inspired in the children appeared contagious. With all of the fun things happening around me I wondered what would happen if only adults were allowed into the park and children stayed home. Would the amusement park be such a fun place to spend a weekend? Can you picture a bunch of middle-aged adults walking from ride to ride, jumping up and down, and having a fun time? No, I cannot imagine such a scene. I do not believe having adults only at an amusement park is a happy situation. Therefore, I must revisit my earlier question: Do children inspire happiness? Yes, we can observe from a different perspective what would happen in certain activities if children were not present. Most parents have experienced some of the happiest times in their lives with the inspiration of their children. Therefore, we must conclude that children do inspire happiness.

Do children inspire happiness? Please describe a situation where you recognized how children inspired happiness in your life.

_____

_____

_____

_____

_____

_____

_____

_____

_____

_____

_____

_____

_____

_____

_____

_____

_____

_____

_____

# YOU DESERVE
# TO BE
# HAPPY

# Employees with Happy Enthusiasm

What happens to some employees who start off with such good attitudes, excited and happy about their new jobs? How do they lose the passion for their jobs and responsibilities? Recently I had the opportunity to meet some employees who were starting new jobs. Their excitement and happiness were unimaginable. As we are often told, a happy employee results in better job performance. As I talked with these employees and thought of the reasons for their excitement and happiness I realized that it was a new experience for them. Since most new employees are looking for something better than their last jobs, it's easy to understand their anticipated happiness.

We strive for better jobs with higher pay to increase our happiness or gain satisfaction. No one applies for a job thinking *I can't wait to be sad at this job,* or, *this is going to be the worst job ever.* As I stated earlier, everyone is searching for happiness or a better situation. One thing that I realized early in my career was that the early days of happiness in a job will soon fade. Why? Did that happiness not really exist? Was it really the *anticipation* of possible happiness, the excitement of believing that happiness could be obtained in a job?

Do most employees start a new job with lots of enthusiasm? Please describe your attitude when you started a new job.

_____

_____

_____

_____

_____

_____

_____

_____

_____

_____

_____

_____

_____

_____

_____

_____

_____

_____

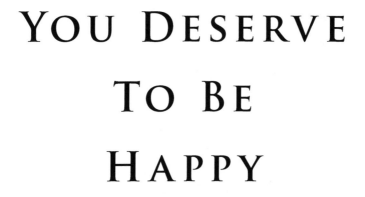

# You Deserve
# To Be
# Happy

# Don't Take My Happiness

Can a person take away our happiness? I recently witnessed an interesting event at my local recreation center in which someone took an individual's happiness. One night I entered the locker room, selected a locker, and started to put my gym clothes on. There weren't many people there, so it was easy to notice a group of young boys walking through the locker room. I thought it was strange that they stopped in front of a bathroom mirror to take pictures and engage in horseplay.

Well, boys will be boys. So I was not surprised when they left the locker room and turned off the lights. First, they turned them on and off, and then I could hear them laughing as they turned off the lights for the last time.

I also heard a man in the locker room shout, "Turn the lights back on!" He muttered, "Those damn kids!" as he turned the lights back on, clearly upset. He was talking to himself and seemed frustrated. When he sat down in front of his locker he pounded on it and slammed the door. It was obvious that those kids had incensed him and ended his happiness for the day. This was ironic because most people go to the gym to enjoy themselves and to obtain some sort of happiness. Why would a person let someone else control their happiness? Well, it appears that everyone should always make a conscious effort to be happy all of the time. When this incident happened, I simply laughed to myself and thought *kids will be kids.* And I never gave it a second thought. I was not going to allow someone or something to control my happiness. If a small situation can control us, what will happen when a more serious situation occurs? Remember, we can control our happiness. No one else should be able to control our actions.

In our modern age of technology and Internet it is easy for us to retrieve videos of people having their happiness taken—people engaging in fights or arguments; just about every type of behavior that will *not* bring them happiness. The other day I viewed a news story about a father of four who crashed into a car, killing someone. The police suspected that he had been drinking and indicated that he would be charged with manslaughter. The man in the crash later stated that he only had two drinks; however, he had exceeded the state's legal limit. Unfortunately, none of this will bring happiness to the father of four. He will think about how he took a life; that he will not be able to see his family; the financial burden he placed on them; the loss of his job and home; countless financial obligations; public embarrassment—and a host of other problems. All because he made a decision that usually results in a bad conscience. Why do people make choices that can result in unhappy conclusions? Is it that we do not believe bad things will happen to us? The evidence is all around us, reported by news outlets every day. We have been witnessing and hearing about car accidents caused by drunken driving for years; however, people still drink and drive. We have also viewed employees stealing money from their employers, being convicted, and spending countless years in prison; however, it still occurs. Witnessing people spending unhappy years in prison has not been a deterrent for this type of behavior. People are still choosing to engage in behavior that will not bring them happiness. Why?

Can someone really take away your happiness, or do you give it away freely? Please describe a situation where someone tried to steal your happiness, or you gave it away.

_____

_____

_____

_____

_____

_____

_____

_____

_____

_____

_____

_____

_____

_____

_____

_____

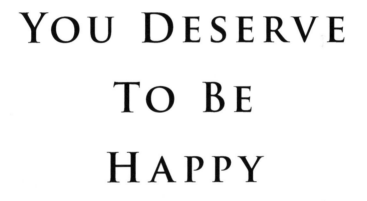

# You Deserve
# To Be
# Happy

# SUMMARY

I am sure that reading and analyzing this book has been an eye-opening experience. Everyone has the awesome power to change situations that makes them unhappy, it's an individual choice. Change it, or complain about it. Hopefully, after reading this book you will choose to change your situation to obtain or maintain happiness. We have discovered many ways to create happiness and prevent unhappiness. Every action has a reaction. For every positive action there is a negative one, and vice-versa. With each action, people experience happy or sad emotions, depending on the situation. Would most people recognize happiness if they did not experience sadness? Or maybe it's more realistic to say that most people recognize happiness because they have witnessed or experienced sadness.

My research has uncovered excellent ways to become happier. One of them is to create happiness by having fun—such as through exercise, which connects our minds and bodies. Being active makes us happier and is good for our physical health. It instantly improves our moods, and can even lift us out of depression. We do not all need to run marathons; there are simple things we can do to be more active each day. In this book we have asked some very important questions, such as, Can happiness be measured by a judge? Will the key to proper measurement begin with the meaning of the word *happiness*?

The problem, of course, is that happiness is used in at least two ways. The first is as an emotion. The second is as an evaluation. Happiness is an aspiration of every human being and can also be a measure of social progress. America's founding fathers declared the inalienable right to pursue happiness for everyone.

The title of this book is *Happiness is a Moving Target*. It does not matter what we currently own, or our economic status. There always is a commercial or media story telling us that we will be happy when we obtain something or change our life status.

Why do we change? It appears that we change because we are all searching for happiness. Can we imagine a world where nothing ever changes, where people stop desiring things? Becoming stagnant in an area of life in which you're unhappy is not a benefit. If a situation is not making you happy, change it. Everyone has the power to change situations that make them unhappy. It's an individual choice. Change it, or complain about it. I choose to change my situation to obtain or maintain happiness. Complaining will not give me the results I desire.

We all want to lead happy lives and want the people we love to be happy, too. But as a society we are not giving happiness enough priority. Despite decades of economic growth we are no happier now than we were sixty years ago. We need to rethink our priorities. The good news is that our actions and choices can affect our happiness. What makes us happy has less to do with our money or possessions than our attitudes and relationships with other people. Happiness is a choice and mind-set. As I've stated, maybe our main purpose in life is to experience minor periods of happiness.

# References

Hellriegel and Slocum, *Organizational Behavior*, Southwestern Cengage learning, Mason OH, 2011.

Jonathan Haidt, *The Happiness Hypothesis*, New York, NY, Perseus Books Group, 2006.

Rich Hanson, *Hardwiring Happiness*, Ebury Publishing, a Random House Group, 2013.

Wicker, Don, *Attitude Is # 1*, Bloomington, IN: AuthorHouse, 2010.

   *Goal Setting: Confidence + Goals = Success*, Bloomington, IN: AuthorHouse, 2008.

   *Job Satisfaction: Fact or Fiction*, Bloomington, IN: AuthorHouse, 2011.

   *Motivation: An Interactive Guide*, Bloomington, IN: AuthorHouse, 2009.

   *Success Is for Everyone*, Bloomington, IN: AuthorHouse, 2012.

   *Why Is It Hard To Find A Job After 50?* Bloomington, IN: AuthorHouse, 2013.

# ABOUT THE AUTHOR

Dr. Don Wicker is a professor of business and management at Brazosport College in Lake Jackson, Texas. He holds a doctoral degree in organization and management with a concentration in leadership. He teaches at the undergraduate and graduate levels, and he has published six books. He has held visiting posts at universities throughout Michigan and Texas since 1999. Other books Dr. Wicker has authored include *Goal Setting*, *Motivation: An Interactive Guide*, *Attitude Is #1*, *Job Satisfaction*, *Success Is for Everyone*, and *Why Is It Hard To Find a Job After 50?* During his twenty-one-year career in business with General Motors Corporation, Dr. Wicker was a senior manager in the areas and departments of accounting, auditing, finance, vehicle sales, service, and marketing.